YO
WELLSPRING
OF
PLENTY

Let go the cupful and have the ocean

by Shaun de Warren

Wellspring Publications

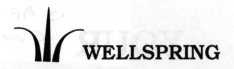

WELLSPRING

Wellspring Publications Limited

46 Cyril Mansions, Prince of Wales Drive
London SW11 4HW. UK

YOUR WELLSPRING OF PLENTY

© Shaun de Warren 1993

Illustrations © Gill Coupland

ISBN: 0-9513520-8-3

Further copies of this and other Wellspring publications
listed on pages 61 to 64 may be obtained from
the publisher or good book stores.

Printed and bound in Great Britain by
BPCC Wheatons Ltd, Exeter

ACKNOWLEDGEMENTS

To those who have guided and inspired me along the way, many of whom I have listed in previous books and to which list I add CBJ and Arnold Patent.

To Denis Vaughan, once again, for his recording and transcription of these lectures for publishing.

To Michael McWhinnie for his generous introduction and valued support and assistance.

To Brian Mayne for all he has done in preparing this book and guiding it to publication.

To Kate Milligan for her editorial assistance.

To Gill Coupland for her design, diagrams and illustrations which bring a brightness and fun to the book.

To all those who choose
to live Prosperously

INTRODUCTION

If someone tells you that—in terms of prosperity, love, joy, peace, happiness and relationships—not only can you *have it all,* but you already *are* it all, you might think him either slightly crazy, or as someone who has found the answers.

I believe Shaun de Warren has found the answers—and this book is for those who want to share them.

In its pages you will find clear directions and signposts to fresh thinking and new beliefs that will enable you to rediscover the magnificence of your real self; to recapture the ecstacy of being vitally alive through *loving yourself* and others, and put you in touch with the abundant riches that are yours, that you deserve, but have somehow lost touch with. These riches are both spiritual and material. For in energy terms there is no difference.

As you read you will open to new insights as well as being reminded of things that you always knew were true. There are no fixed rules, methods, chants, mystical rites, hidden secrets. The process, if you let it, is as simple and natural as living itself. It all works for everyone. But you will pay special attention to those words, phrases and paragraphs that jump off the page and seem specifically written for you. They probably were.

Choose as you will from this a la carte menu of plenty. You can eat whole courses or nibble small bites. You will find it all deliciously nourishing at many different levels. With Shaun at your table you will be encouraged to try new things, take some steps, see others in a different light, make new choices—and, above all, to enjoy every abundant moment, knowing that it really is *all yours for the asking.*

At Shaun's meetings and courses, through his books and tapes many people's lives have been renewed and transformed. Shaun does not do it *to* or *for* anyone. He does it *with* everyone—in a loving relationship designed to help us all become more of who we really are, have more of what we truly want and do all that we want to do.

I am able to write this because when I first met Shaun,—warm, intelligent, caring, spiritual and charming as he is—I frankly suspected that he might, underneath it all, be slightly crazy. But when his advice to me worked—time, after time, after time—my scepticism disappeared, my life expanded wonderfully—and I found a very real friend.

I know it can be the same for you. So turn the pages and prepare to enjoy the health, wealth, happiness, peace, love, joy and right relationships that you can create as you tap into you own *inexhaustible well of plenty*.

Mike McWhinnie.
Camberley 1992.

IT'S ALL YOURS
FOR THE ASKING

There are some universal principles, and ways of
applying them, to bring to ourselves the things
which we have always wanted.

The first principle is that everything is energy.
Everything is vibratory in nature ... I'm energy, you're
energy, this page is energy and the light on it is energy.
They are all the same energy, not different types of energy.
The only difference between them is their rates of
vibration.
When we understand that, we understand that we are
everything else that is, that we are the universe itself,
that each is the other.
The only thing that makes us different is that rate at
which we vibrate.
It makes sense to recognize that what we do to each other,
we do to ourselves ... and that what we do to
ourselves we do to each other.
In a sense, we are all the same vibratory energy.
If I start judging someone else, who am I really judging,
since that "someone else" is also me?
I am projecting something, and my projection is a
judgement on myself.
*If I were to give up my judgements on myself, I would
not need to judge others.*

*The second principle is that the base of everything is
love.*
If love is the base of everything, then everything is
motivated into form through love—not through stress
or through trying hard, or through any clever occult
principles.
Everything comes from love.
You and I are love ... and we've probably heard this many
times.

We may hear and understand it intellectually, but until it
    reaches our heart, and we recognize the truth of it,
    nothing changes.
If you have been stuck in your life, getting more of the
    same, feeling it doesn't matter what you do or that, no
    matter what system you follow, you will still end up
    the same, then you have not allowed this truth to land.

Also true is: *"We are perfect just the way we are."*
You are perfect just the way you are ... and I am perfect
    just the way I am.
One of the errors we make is in trying to change people.
We have a picture of how "more perfect" it could be for
    that person ... that "that person would be more
    perfect if they responded to me in a different way, if
    they didn't do something they do, or if they were to
    give up some addiction".

We do everything we can to change them.
This violates the very law of perfection: *everything is*
    perfect just the way it is.
We cannot see the greater plan, we can only see our
    narrow picture.
So, in this moment, the way it is is perfect.
There is nothing we have to change in ourselves to be
    perfect.
If we acknowledge our essential perfection, and the
    perfection of each other—"You are perfect the way
    you are. I set you free. There is nothing I want to do
    to change you. I love you the way you are", we can
    then, within that freedom, change our perceptions
    about ourselves.
The only thing that changes is our perception ... which is
    why we are told the world is an illusory universe.
The world is not the illusion, the illusion is our perception
    of ourselves.
The change we make is in the way we see
    ourselves ... and we come nearer to the recognition
    that who we are is divine love.

We may not feel very loving, and we may not see loving
people around us, but that is because we have an
error in our thinking—our perception has not been
fully realized in the truth.

The changes we make are to open ourselves to receive the
truth, the beauty, the love, the life, the joy and the
prosperity of who we are.

Prosperity is our natural self.

Love is our natural self.

If prosperity is our natural self, and we are not
prosperous, it must mean we are working extremely
hard to keep ourselves from receiving it.

People who work night and day just to cover their debts
think this viewpoint is crazy.

Who we are is naturally prosperous.

When we are not prosperous, we are resisting prosperity
at some level of our being.

When we are not loving, when we are not having a
wonderful time, we are resisting the truth of our
being at some level.

This turns the whole thing on its face.

The normal way of functioning is, "This is a hard world
and I have got to earn a crust to make my way in
this hard world."

*The next principle is that the universe is a mutually
supporting system.*

The universe is designed to support everything in it ... and
that includes us as well as everything else, including
all of the animals, trees, grubs, fishes and things
which fly.

Why do we feel unsupported when the universe has been
designed to mutually support us?

Why do we have to struggle and effort in life, to put up
with the things we do not want, and not have those
things which we do want?

What is going wrong?

When we acknowledge that this is a mutually supportive
   universe, we also acknowledge each person is here to
   support each other.
The missing link is that we often try to go it alone.
We try to make our life go it alone.
We resist the support of others.
We resist the feedback of the universe.

We can only do it together.

If we are going to make the changes in the world and in
   our own lives, the only way is if we do it
   together—the way it is designed.
Support groups and supporting each other does not mean
   doing it for each other, paying for others or carrying
   them in some way.
My supporting you means that you have my consciousness
   and my intention that your life works out exactly in
   the way that is right for you.
You do not have my support in destroying yourself.
You have my support in your life blossoming to its fullness.
If only everybody were to give each other this support,
   rather than remain in conflict or try to be better than
   each other—the lavatory cleaner will support the
   manager and the manager will support the company
   chairman and vice versa. We must let go of being
   "better than" and become equal as human beings.
In equality we can truly give and receive.

*Are there any of these principles I am not using in my
   life?*
Is there anything here that I stick on?
Am I trying to be better than other people?
Am I not giving unconditional love?
Am I not loving openly and freely?
*Is my love based on 'I'll love you if you love me. If you
   do not do what I want you to, then don't expect me
   to love you'.*
*... Are these what are stopping me from finding the joy
   in togetherness?*

The old games of control and manipulation do not bring
   us any joy.
We must clear them away, so we can truly ask.
We cannot ask in an environment of 'not willing to
   receive'.
We cannot ask in an atmosphere that says, 'this is a bad
   world', or 'I don't deserve it', because the asking falls
   on barren ground.
... We must begin to unravel our relationship with ourself.

*The first and only relationship we really have is that
   with the divine—the universe—they are the same.*

Am I in conflict with the universe?
Am I this small pea that is separate from it?
Do I have to struggle to prove something?
Do I have to get some 'success' under my belt, some
   degrees and other things in order to be worthy and to
   have the things I want?

If we straighten this key relationship out, we can start
   looking at the others.
Most of us start the other way around.
We try to 'handle' relationships with one another when we
   have not resolved our relationship with the universe.
When we are in a belief that we are this 'separate thing'
   trying to have a relationship, we will not have any
   movement.
It is better to first discover our relationship with the
   universe.

We could describe the universe as infinite love and
   endless energy.
Where is our place in it?
Do I align with that, saying, 'That's OK with me! I'll be
   infinite love and endless energy', or do we say,
   'That's simplistic! I haven't lived this long and gone
   through all of the things I have been through for you
   to tell me THIS!'

We have the choice.

We can be willing to let go, trust the universe, and
      acknowledge it is all designed as a mutual support
      system.
It is infinite love.
I am the same as it.
It is how I am in relationship.
I can now walk down the street with a smile on my face,
      knowing that the universe is here to support and love
      me, and I can look at my relationship with myself:

Do I hate myself?
Do I feel unworthy?
Do I feel rejected?
Do I feel less than other people?
Do I feel stupid?

Notice all of the judgements we place on ourself.
The world is going to be the way the pictures we have of it
      come out of our mind.
The pictures are determined by the relationship we have
      with ourself.

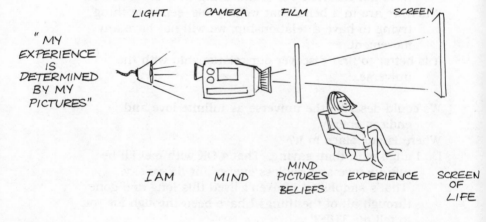

Endless courses and training programmes encourage
people to love themselves.
We understand intellectually that we must learn to love
ourself.
But when we learn to look into our feelings, which is the
key, IS that how we really feel?

The route to a relationship with ourself from the divine
and out into the world is through our feelings.
It is in our feelings that we find the purpose of our life.
Purpose is a direction.
Purpose is not a thing, like a goal.
A goal is, "I want that nice new car", and, by putting my
attention on it, I move towards it.
Purpose does not have this physicality or thingness about
it.
Purpose is a direction which is endless—a direction we
are drawn to.

The way to encourage people to get to that purpose is to
let them ask themselves, "What are the things I really
love doing? "
Taking one of these, such as, "I really love being with
loving people", or "I really love eating in nice
restaurants, walking in the country, or
sailing" ... when we are doing the thing we love
doing, how do we feel?
The key is the feeling we want to have when we are doing
these things.
If you really love being with intimate people, you may say
you want to feel intimate, belonging, a oneness,
happy, joyful, in communication, with a sense of
communion, peaceful and at ease.
The external event brings the feelings we want.
We may take ten different things we love doing and arrive
back through those ten to the same feeling.
Appreciating this can change our perspective on life.
Our purpose is to feel the way we want to: prosperous,
powerful, beautiful, sexy, or wonderful ...

Life can take a new slant:

—"I did not come here just to get by", or
—"I did not come here just to have a job, struggle for fifty
     years, retire and drop dead. That is not what life is
     about".

Purpose is about bringing the feelings we want here.
If I love feeling really intimate in a relationship, one of the
     aspects of my purpose is to bring that intimacy.
If I enjoy prosperity and feel prosperous in one of the ten
     or so activities I have listed, one of my purposes is to
     bring prosperity.
None of our purpose feelings have thingness about
     them—they are qualities.

We become the bringer of gifts.
The feelings I want to feel, I want to share.
I can only share the feelings I want to feel with other
     people, which is why it is something we do together.
If you were to ask, "What is the principle behind having
     fun?", the answer is: "Doing it together".
Have you tried having fun by yourself? It runs out of
     steam very quickly.
The joy is in having fun together, doing something
     together that is fun.
The same is true of purpose: we can only fulfill our
     purpose with other people
Purpose as referred to here includes everybody ...

"Because I want to feel and be prosperous,
     and since I am energy
          and you are energy
               and there is no difference between us,
     it must also be true that I want you to be
          prosperous."

We cannot have prosperity, we cannot have love, and we
     cannot have peace unless they are for everybody.

The truth of it is that we can only have those things we
  are willing to give.
We begin to see some of the aspects we want to look at in
  our own lives which have to do with receiving and
  with asking for what we want.
Asking is fascinating . . . people rarely ask—they demand,
  or tell you what they would like.
People may say, "I would really like to come and see you",
  but never take the next step . . . people seem
  embarrassed to ask.
Instead of asking, we demand, or "don't ask", and expect
  others to think that we DID ask.
We often sell ourselves short by not actually asking for
  what we really want.

When you ask, you must be willing to receive a
  "no" . . . but you are not likely to receive a "yes"
  unless you ask.
We can ask each other, and we can ask of the universe.

*We will never receive anything, until we have already
  given it to ourselves.*
Whatever it is that you want, give it to yourself!

So long as it is not damaging anyone else, or taking
  something from someone else, give what you want to
  yourself.
How can we expect others to love us, if we do not love
  ourselves?
How can we expect others to acknowledge us, if we do not
  acknowledge ourselves.

People do unto us as we do unto ourselves.

When we first do the giving to ourselves, we find we
  naturally give of the same to others.
So, in asking, we can ask of each other and support each
  other in our asking, as well as in our giving and
  receiving.

We can also ask inwardly—just making the request.
The way to make this kind of request is to form a picture
of already having received it.

When we hold a picture of already having received what
we want, not only mentally, but also in our hearts, so
that it is actually embodied and we have that sense
of "Yes!", then the request will be answered.

What we can see is ours.
If we can see a negative world, that is the world we get.
If we see a world heading for destruction, that is the world
we get.
Our world is as we see it ... *and only we can change the
way we see it.*

Meditation is another way of asking.

Meditation essentially means being alert, forming that relationship with the universe, or the divine, through surrendering to it and becoming part of it.

We surrender the negative thoughts, our judgements and evaluations, and come to peace and ease.

In peace and ease we come to gratitude.

In gratitude we recognize that everything that comes to us is a gift for our benefit.

When we are willing to surrender to that gratitude, everything in the universe shifts.

When we surrender, instead of fighting things, trying to push them away and being 'dis-integrated' from them, we receive them and integrate them into ourselves.

When we acknowledge and receive, the gift is given ... far greater gifts than we could ever ask for ...

Miracles happen when we are willing to surrender 'our' way of doing it.

'Our' way of doing it has led us this far, to how we are experiencing things now.

We need to take a step and to enrol the universe itself.

When we truly ask, with nothing in the way of our receiving, such as a belief about ourself which negates our having it, the gift is already given.

Let's take a look at two different people:

One accepts and acknowledges the universe as a mutually supporting system based on love, which is just an energy.

The other thinks life is hard and a struggle.

The one who thinks life is a struggle gets out of bed and finds everything wrong: the cat's sick, the children are screaming, breakfast is burnt, no buses, waiting for hours, getting more angry with the world, finally gets to work, the coffee's cold, piles of papers, a day of struggling through and hating every minute of it, impossible to get a bus home, and, when home, screaming at the wife and children.

The next day he gets up and the cat's made a mess ...

The other one thinks the universe is a mutually
supportive system: he gets up, wonders "What
miracles are going to happen today?", "What
wonderful new people will I meet today?", "How easy
and joyful today is going to be." It becomes easy.
Breakfast is wonderful, outside the door, someone
offers him a lift to work, his desk is clear, someone
brings him coffee and newspapers and says, "We've
dealt with all of your stuff today and you can have
the day off"—he goes home and plays, opens the mail
to find that his share certificates have multiplied in
value ... everything is wonderful, including a lovely
dinner.

The next morning he wakes up and wonders, "What
miracles today?" ...

Both have the same set of circumstances, but different
perceptions ... and both of these people are perfect
just the way they are.

The only difference between them is in their perceptions of
the universe and in their perceptions of
themselves ...

Only we can make the shift—no-one can make it for us.
We can be encouraged to do it, supported in doing it, but
only WE can do it.
The game of life is to see how wonderful we can have it.
Can it be more wonderful today than yesterday?
How much more wonderful could it be tomorrow?

Someone came to me who said her life had blossomed and
she could not see how things could be more
wonderful.

I advised her to keep going, and she returned the following
week to say, "You're right. It is even *more*
wonderful!"

When you start hitting the ceiling of wonderful, keep going.
That is really the journey of life, opening to more and
more of the wonder.

We cannot do it alone.

The message of this decade is to do it together, in
partnership, supporting one another, using every
opportunity to form networks or groups bonded by
love and supporting each other's lives.

It has been said that, if everybody were to co-operate, the
poorest man on this planet would be richer than the
richest man on this planet within ten years.

We usually think that if we co-operate, become part of
everybody else, we will lose something.

We have a feeling that, "I've struggled for all this and I am
not going to let it go. It's mine!"

When we are willing to let that go and move into a
relationship of moving energy—of being to being and
of mutual support—we could do in a tenth of the time
what now takes a full day . . . we could spend 90% of
the time lying on the beach.

All of the concepts and principles I explore are so that life
becomes easier and more wonderful.

Life takes a step when we discover new and deeper levels
of the truth of ourselves and of the nature of being.

We bring here a whole new state for the enjoyment of all.

These discoveries which we make together make life
become a continual party to which we are all invited.

Life is not serious.

Seriousness makes life hard.

Life is a play, a joy, a delight and, the more delighted we
are, the more enlightened we are—and the easier it
becomes.

21

When you meet enlightened people, you find they are not
heavy with intellectual principles and concepts—they
are light! They play. They have fun ... and, yet, in
their playfulness, remarkable things happen.
Enlightened people do not avoid the real issues in their
playfulness—they address them, tickle them, and say,
"Come on. You come and play, too".
If enough people were to play, to truly enjoy and be in
delight, the real "issues" of life would disappear.
"Issues" in life only appear because of our belief in them.
Crime only exists because of our belief in scarcity, and our
belief that someone else has something that we want.
As we begin to love ourselves more and to see that we
already have it all, these beliefs change.

*It is not a question of acquiring it—it is a matter of
expressing it.*
*We have right now and here all of the love, the joy and
peace that we really are ... and we can open to it
and ask for it to be experienced.*

We have the power of choice every moment of every day.
We can actually choose to change a sense that we are
being held by a negative feeling.
We can step out of the old belief and choose anew ... if the
old belief pops in again, keep choosing until there is
enough of the new feeling for it to have its own life
and move forward.
It helps to have the bonding and support of people who
actually support us in our new choices.
With enough support for us in our new choice, we
recognize the truth of us is love and innocence and
there is no stain on us—the only stain was a belief
we had.

Everything is to me as I see it.
*If my attitude is to see this world as being my enemy,
here in some way to get me, that "I haven't got the
time to deal with all these wretched people" and
"I've GOT to do my work", this is the world I get.*

If my attitude is, "this is a hostile world, here to hold me up", then the cat will get sick and I will have to clear it up.
Everything responds to the message I put out.

Animals reflect their owners very much—a sick animal usually means the owner has difficulties, too.
If we are 'off', it means our vibration is off, as in sickness—we are still fine, perfect just where we are—we are just 'off'.

It is senseless to do anything other than what we love doing—a total waste of time.
Love what we do, even though it may not be exactly what we want at this time—the way out of it is to love it, rather than resist it.
This takes courage.
If we are in a job or a relationship we do not like, it changes when we transform it by loving the job or the person.

Loving our projection of ourself is not the aim—it is getting back to the acknowledgement that we ARE love.
The aim is not puffery, inflating the ego.
Inflating the ego is separation.

In asking for something, ask for the precise thing, not the money for it.
We do not need to know the mechanism through which it works—all we do is ask.
Ask for what we want, rather than demand; and accept what we get as being perfect for now.
"Seek ye first the Kingdom of Heaven and all else will be added unto you."

When we are happy, at peace and in our oneness, everything will just wellspring from that anyway—so ask for that!

23

Meditation

I know that no-one will give me anything until I have
    first given it to myself.

I am the source of all the gifts to me
    By giving what I want to myself
        As a gift in consciousness
            And, by opening to receive that gift,
                I open myself to asking.

I ask from the Divine and from others what I want,
    Knowing what I ask for is freely available
        And is not harmful to another.

And being willing to participate in the manifesting
    process,
        By holding the vision and taking the
            necessary steps,
                All I ask for can be mine
                  and is mine already.

LOVING YOURSELF

**The Alpha and Omega of life is that there is only
love ... and resistance to love.**

Imagine a circle.
Outside of the circle is love, which is an infinity.
We cannot describe it intellectually, because the very
  description of it would move it into form.
Outside the circle we have oneness; inside it twoness and
  form.

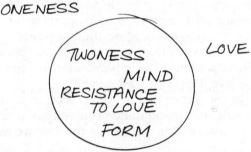

Wherever mind exists there is twoness.
Wherever love exists there is oneness.
*The experience of love is nothing which we can truly
  describe.*

The prime place to experience love is in the heart.
Love starts as a feeling in the heart, and develops to a
  sensation in every cell of the body.
Every cell is a complete universe in itself, every cell
  experiences love and is able to express love.
As there is only love, everything that is within the circle,
  which we call 'not-love', is resistance to love; such
  things as jealousy, fear, pain, sorrow, resentment and
  all the rest of them.
This gives us a clear distinction between loving and
  resisting loving.

Why would we resist love?

25

Why do we feel the sensations of anger, greed, hurt, upset,
and feelings of separation, if all there is is love—and
we all like feeling love?
Can you imagine there is anyone on the planet who would
not like feeling love?
What is this craziness we get into?
Is there something that is not love?
These resistances to love are not something different—it is
not 'love' over here and then something else called
'all the other things'.
When we find ourselves in 'all the other things', we think
we somehow have to battle our way to love, or try to
persuade love to come to us by praying, or whatever
we do to get something we think we need.
We sit in ourselves thinking, "I am this fear-bound,
pathetic person. I feel separate, lonely, and I want
some love. How can I get some?"
If we are in the 'other things', the answer is to try to
persuade and manipulate people—have a drama, get
sick ... maybe *this* will get us the love we want.

There are people who create a lot of drama in their lives,
and who think that, by having these sorts of
experiences.
They will be loved and will get the attention, sympathy
and pity they want ... but it does not work.
They do not feel anything and cannot experience the
feelings they want, because the drama is not true for
them.
It is yet another resistance to love.

People whose whole lives are about suffering are also
about resistance to love.
Suffering is pain, and pain lives in the small circle of
twoness.
So why would I want to suffer?
The answer for most people is that they think that by
suffering they are going to get more love—maybe in
the hereafter—they think they have some sort of

investment in something beyond what they are feeling right now.

Anything which is based in the future cannot be love.

A love in the future cannot exist—both past and future belong to the mind, to twoness.

In separateness we live in the past and in the future.

We cannot look to the past and have love.

Remembering is a mental exercise.

Any love we experience is a present reality, right here and now.

Our mind divides 'love' and all the 'other things', and when we do that, we try to resolve the 'other things' by putting our attention on them, rather than recognizing that all of these 'other things' are, in fact, parts of love.

'Other things' are just ways in which we are being reminded that we are witholding our love.

If I am being jealous, I am closing down my love for someone, because I think they have something I want and do not have.

When I get jealous, I feel bad . . . and bad things happen.

What I put out, I get back.

We are the centre of our own universe.

There is only love.

I am expressing from me, through the filters of my thinking . . . so whatever I think or see over there is me.

If I see 'bad' over there, it is the 'bad' in me which I am looking at.

If I see problems, or people putting me down, that is how I am feeling about myself.

The love I am talking about is about loving ourselves.

We cannot love the universe, the world, or the people in it until we begin to be good to ourselves.

27

Some wonder, "Is that not egotistical? Is it not better if we put ourselves last in everything?"

The self we are dealing with here is not the personality self and has nothing to do with puffing ourselves up, or loving the vainess that we are.

Who we are is not the personality

This self is a recognition that *This* is my source.

If *This* is my source, the source of love, then I can acknowledge that.

This is the step.

I am a loving being.

My source is love.

I come from the same fountain as you.

I may have all sorts of ideas and opinions, and may have made many decisions about myself based on my past performance.

We find we have judged ourselves and decided that we are worthy or unworthy, good or bad, intelligent or stupid.

As we make these judgements on ourselves we close down, and we are unable to receive love, or to acknowledge that we are love ... because we are looking from the mind side of the circle.

We have not taken the step.

Just step backwards and see the mind now presented in front of you and the feelings, like hurt and loneliness, which are here to be examined.

We can find we can experience feelings as if they are a passing wind or cloud, and that we are the space that contains that wind or cloud—the space that contains those feelings ... they are not who we are.

When we think the feelings are who we are and feel we are being buffetted from all sides with the pain, it means we are putting out more of the same.

When we are able to step back and be aware of these thoughts, we find that at the bottom of them all is love.

There is nothing that we can think and nothing that we
      can feel which is not, taken to its ultimate, love—just
      as all matter, taken to its ultimate, is energy.
Every feeling and every emotion we have is either
      love . . . or a witholding of love.

Instead of being a pea in the universe, chasing around
      trying to find some love, we find ourselves on the
      other side of the circle.

This is ME, and I recognize that all of these things are
      going on inside me.
Instead of chasing around in stress trying to solve
      problems, trying to find the solution to life with our
      tiny pea brains, and going after those things which
      we think will make us whole, we recognise that "I am
      the wholeness".

There is nothing I have to do to be whole.
There is nowhere to go, as I am the infinite.
I am perfect the way I am.
All there is to do is to experience what is going on and to
      make the changes.
It is not me that has to change . . . it is the perceptions
      that I have.

People have difficulty in accepting that they are fine . . . yet,
  when we go deep into ourselves—perhaps in
  meditation, we feel fine, warm, loving, safe and
  without stress . . .
But afterwards we rise up, take on the mental perceptions
  that we have, and the stress and problems come back
  again.
The problems that we have are self-created—out of our
  thinking and our perceptions.
We change the perception—NOT the base, which is
  fine—WE are loving beings.
We are loving beings . . . and we look in what we
  think . . . and in what we feel.

The evidence which shows us our thinking and feeling is
  how life is for us.
We might say, "Life's OK" and our thinking and feeling is
  at that level.
We may be acting at a chicken level . . . when we could be
  eagles.
'Eagle' is available, if we are willing to look at it and see
  how we measure up to it.

30

Who we are is the same—the same as people who are
    having a wonderful, successful and loving time.
We are not different at our base.
It is not that the stars have decided we should have a bad
    time.
We can explain away the state we are in ('God has really
    got it in for me!'), or we can change it.
Wonderful explanations change nothing.

The mirror of life will show us what we need to change.
Each of us is our own laboratory for discovery—there is
    no "the answer".
You are the answer.
Each one of us is the key and can bring about the
    changes.
Change the negative, fear-based pictures.
Fear is faith in a negative result.

Love and hate are the same energy, so hate is 100%
    witholding of love.
We absolutely deny any amount of love for a person we
    hate.
The only person who suffers from hate is ourselves.
As we send out hate, we receive it back; so we only send it
    out if we hate ourselves.
We only send out what we feel about ourselves.
The message given is the message received.

As we see, we see ourselves.

MIRROR

MIRROR

MIRROR

MIRROR

ME

Anger, greed and jealousy are just witholdings of love.

Love is freedom, a gift, an emanation from the divine,
which we experience through feeling.

We give love as a gift—others do not have to *do* something
for it.

"If you betray my love, I will never trust you again" is
control and a 'giving to get', not love.

We cannot betray or damage love, so in *true* love we set
people free—and in that freedom we also are able to
receive.

We are like certain flowers which can only receive rain
when they are in the right position—if we are not in
that position, we cannot also give.

Each of us is a giving and receiving of love.

Our usual conditioning, which encourages us to think we
are bad, wrong and sinners, is based on fear.

Almost all of most lives are based on fear—a witholding of
love.

Even mothers and fathers keep telling their children they
are wrong.

A babysitter says to a howling baby, "You *bad* girl!" and
it all starts—and is compounded when the great
churches reinforce a sense of sin and guilt.

Although there may be some very loving people in the
system, it seems all to be about getting from "bad" to
"good".

Traditional education systems and governments are also
fear-based.

We are in a world which lives in fear, and our situation is
compounded by having a death sentence hanging
over our heads—how do we get out of this trap?

The fears and judgements are all the mind speaking—all
beliefs built by man, designed to control and keep
people in order.

Beliefs are only beliefs, not necessarily real.

Beliefs are only structures in our thinking and we can
change them.

We have already challenged and changed beliefs like, "The world is flat", "You cannot run a mile in four minutes", and "You cannot get to the moon".
We are now looking at ones like: "We cannot have a world without hunger" and "We cannot have a world without death".

If there is only love, which is immortal, and every cell of our body is love, why does it have to disappear?
We are only at a chicken level in our ignorance—we have not begun to fly with the eagles.

Could it be that we are eagles and never knew it?

Could it be that if we change some perceptions we may find amazing new realities like, for example, that we can be together forever?

It is a reality that we are together forever—we have not mastered it physically yet, but that is coming.
Once we get a taste of this, would we not want to be a lot nicer to those around us?
Would this not make it worth cleaning up a few relationships?
While we cannot get rid of relationships, we *can* dissolve the witholds of love between us by opening our heart, forgiving the others, getting to that place of gratitude for them and *feeling* good about them, as we are together forever.

Loving ourself doesn't mean loving this piece here—it means loving everybody, as everybody IS ourself.
Just as there are billions of cells in this body, there are billions of people.
Each is just a reproduction of the other... going out in consciousness.
In loving myself, I am also giving everybody else freedom to be themselves... I am no longer trying to change others.

33

So we say, "You are perfect just the way you are. There is
   nothing I have to do, or want to do, to change you.
   All I want is for you to know that, and to express
   yourself truly to yourself, and not have to hide or
   withold yourself through fear".

At the moment the world is going through the phase of
   changing from opposition and conflict into
   cooperation and partnership.
We are beginning to realise that we *are* one
   another—irretrievably interconnected.
This realization is just beginning to come; at a local level
   in relationships and at a global level between
   nations.
Love is found in partnership.
We start off with "You are the source of my love, so I am
   always looking to you to be loving me. When I do not
   see that happening, I feel I am unloved."
We can get to a level where we recognize that we are the
   source of our love, and know that, if we are not
   feeling love, we are not giving any.
Anyone who is being critical of their partner is lost in how
   they see the other.
The way we see our partners is the way they are for us.
How we see our partners is how we see ourselves, because
   if we were not that way, we would not see it 'over
   there'—we would see a loving human being.
While we do not have to like everybody, have dinner with
   them or spend our lives with them, we can still love
   them.
Loving our partners includes loving all of those aspects of
   them we think should be different.
The best way to have someone change is to let them be
   the way they are, as their essence is love, anyway.

*Everything comes down to relationships, which is
learning to love unconditionally.*

34

If you do not have the love, money, relationships, or job
that you want, just check: are you giving it to
yourself?
The way to give things to yourself is to acknowledge that
you have them.
We live at a beggar level, not acknowledging who we truly
are—when we pretend we are princes and princesses,
we may realize the truth.
The things we truly want are feelings, which are available
to us right now if we acknowledge them and do not
withold our love.
The moment we release our love, we begin to feel them.
As we slip into meditation, letting go of our problems, we
begin to feel love again.

If two people have been together physically for a time,
there is an astral envelope around them, so they feel
a sort of separation at a vital level if they try to
break up.
When we come to a completion, an "I love you, and good
luck, have a wonderful life. I am always here to be
your loving, supportive friend", then we find that they
and we feel perfectly free ... and when we see them, it
is as if there had never been any separation—the
place we were at together is always there—we always
have that feeling with them.
Even if we do not meet them again physically, we can
have that same feeling ... we can feel it in ourselves.

We are beginning to sense that any feeling we have is a
loving feeling.
Some of our feelings are a 'witholding love' feeling, but
they are all the same feeling, although we may call
them different names.

*My purpose in life is to feel and express love in the way
that most attracts me.*

35

Life is a never-ending wheel, a spinning top, unless we
    have purpose.
When we begin to look at that purpose, we may not get
    our life purpose first time around, but we might get
    our "what's our next phase (month or year) -what do
    I want to express more of in my life?"—THIS is how
    we can get to purpose.
"What would I like to feel more like this year?"
The feelings that we want tend to be love, joy, prosperity,
    more expressive, more giving and receiving, more
    harmony and wholeness.
We create our life out of our beingness, out of our love for
    love.

So I must let go of the stress, as I cannot be creative when
    I am being stressful.
Stress and creativity are opposites.
I relax in order to get in touch with my creativity.
If I want to be more prosperous, I get in touch with that
    part of me which feels naturally prosperous—and I
    cannot do this if I am in stress.
Stressful thinking is scarcity thinking.
If I relax, get in touch with the prosperous feeling, and let
    it flow from that, I get in touch with a whole
    wellspring of thoughts and ideas of things I can do
    which will ultimately lead to the physical
    manifestation of that which I want to
    experience—prosperity in this case.

If I want to experience more love, I give and receive more
    love—there is no other way I can do it.
How can I love the people around me more?
I can give up judging them, send loving thoughts to them,
    see them well and happy, see them loving and in
    loving relationships, see them having a wonderful
    life ... AND be willing to receive their love for me

    ... and, guess what?!

    I begin to feel more love in my life.

Now we begin to move to that purpose which we have.

All of the things we want are inherent in us right
      now—we do not have to go and get them, we just
      have to unshackle what is in the way.
We transform in ourselves the things "out there" which
      are in the way of us feeling what we want to feel.
All of those negative feelings which we speak of are the
      very things we want, except that we are holding onto
      them in a negative way, rather than transforming
      them and returning them back to the space we
      started with.
Love, ease, prosperity and creativity are our domain—and
      it exists at the consciousness level, not at the Beta
      level—an eyes-open, walking around, stressful
      'dealing with the world' state—but rather when we
      sink down into ourselves and move into an Alpha, or
      deeper meditative, state.
We begin to get in touch with a part of ourself where we
      will find these things.
Their domain is in contemplation, meditation, being with
      yourself and allowing those things to emerge in you.
If we have a thousand things going on in our head, how
      can new ideas, thoughts and feelings come through?
We are turning it around from this scatty external
      existence to allowing these great things to emerge
      from within.

A seed becomes a tree because something comes from
      within.
A seed just grows until, one day, it becomes a mighty oak.
If humble seeds can become mighty oaks, can *we* not do
      more?
We do not do more, because we have lost our connection
      with that natural essence, our self within, which has
      the knowledge of how we can become our own mighty
      oak.
Being on purpose is being who we truly are.
Being on purpose is something we do step by step.

If we want to feel more love, start now, then check again
     in six weeks time and add more ease, or more
     prosperity... little by little we begin to open
     ourselves.
Our talents begin to shine.
We find new talents—new abilities we never knew we
     had—coming because we now allow ourselves to move
     from the inside as a gift to others.

We cannot do it alone.
We do it together.
We support one another in finding our *own* wellspring.
We support one another to keep each other moving
     forward in the most powerful way.

Meditation

I now see others as expressions of myself and, by
     loving them, I love myself.

As I love myself, I love the Divine.
As I love the Divine, I love myself.
As I love myself, I love others.

I see now that there is only love and allow my heart to
     guide me in my daily actions.

TAPPING INTO YOUR INEXHAUSTIBLE WELL OF PLENTY

God did not say, "Let us just have a couple of apples
     and a pear."
God said, "Let there be plenty."
And there IS plenty.

If there IS plenty, why do we not experience it that way?
What can we do to allow the expression of that plenty to
     be an experience in our lives?
Most people know the principles, but the key is integrating
     them into our lives.
What *is* it that we actually have to do to, or undo, in order
     that we can experience the life that we truly want?
Deep inside, all of us know the life that we truly want.

We may not know what we want to *do*, but we know what
     we want to *feel*.

*We want to feel in touch with the universe, happy,
     loving, free, peaceful, in touch with prosperity . . .
     and at ease.*

How come life is not the way we want it to be?
What would it take for it to be that way?
The truth is that we start from the state of beingness that
     we all are and come into the mind, into our
     thinkingness.
We come from our infinite source, go into the mind and
     then we forget.
We forget that we are the infinite beingness.
We think we are the mind.
When we live our lives in thoughts, everyone and
     everything becomes a thought for us.

39

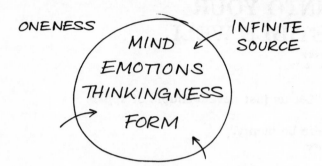

ONENESS   MIND   INFINITE
EMOTIONS   SOURCE
THINKINGNESS
FORM

BEINGNESS

"COMING FROM
BEINGNESS
INTO
FORM"

As I am the oneness, whatever I see 'out there' is me.
Whatever I think about 'someone else' is me.
Whatever I feel about 'them' is me, too.
I look 'out there' and try to change my life.
I know that I want love, money, happiness, relationships
    and I go out into the world to try to get them.
I do all the things that rational thinking tells me to do.

Universities are full of rational thinkers who have all the
    answers ... but change nothing.
If philosophies worked, this world would be a wonderful
    place.
If all those thousands of books which have been written
    on how we should do it worked, we would be doing it.
I have read the books and I know the principles.
Why is it not happening?

We forget who we are.
We forget we are the infinite.
We think we are the mind, which lives in duality, not in
    oneness.

We forget when we are in the surface mind.
The surface mind does not really know, as it is only about
    5% of our mind ... and possibly less.

40

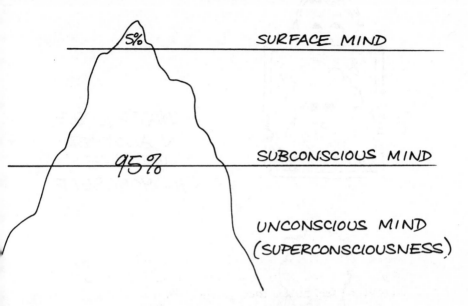

"5% OF US, AT MOST, IS ABOVE THE SURFACE"

We think our surface minds are who we are: "I'm awake,
    my eyes are open and I know exactly what is going
    on in the world."
What I am trying to do is control it.
If everything around me comes to me and fits my
    particular nuttiness, THEN I can have what I want.
But when I get it, I do not like it, because I do not feel
    good about it.
The mind tries to control.
We may get this wonderful relationship, and yet find we
    are trying to control it all the time.

People in relationship want each other to change.
They say, "If only he (or she) would change, my life would
    be wonderful!"
But he (or she) is not going to change, because "they" are
    you.
There is only one.

41

"WHAT YOU SEE
IN ANOTHER
YOU SEE
IN YOURSELF "

Everything you see is you, so what is 'over there' is you.
When we say "He/She must change", what we are actually
    saying is, "I must change".

*It is madness to think that your world can change
    without yourself changing.*

If we do not change, we will ALWAYS get the same.
If we do not change, NOTHING shifts, we may just get new
    and more clever devices to hide behind, new ways of
    keeping ourselves from the truth...
We keep ourselves from the truth in the mind by the
    things we believe, our valuations, our judgements,
    rationalisations, analysis and by everything that, for
    us, has positive-negative aspects.

*The mind does not know harmony—it is trying to find it,
    to find the balance at the centre.*

We *have* mind—we are *not* it.
Once we realize we are not someone trying to get out of
the mind, we just notice there is mind.

"STEPPING OUT OF THE MIND"

Notice the mind is like a computer, stored with
information.
I walk around like an empty space with this great big
computer .. but I blame the world for not relating to
me the way I want it to, and for not giving me the
things I think I should have, when I am the person
who programmed this computer.

I did it!

If I change the programme here, it will change out there.

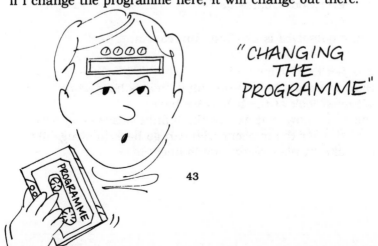

"CHANGING
THE
PROGRAMME"

43

Take responsibility now.

Recognize there is just the one mind.

We like to think there are many minds, because the mind
likes to fragment everything.

The mind sees all the divisions and separations in life.

It only knows the divisions and cannot see or experience
the unity yet.

If we live in the division, we work hard to try to bring
everything together.

Once we are in unity, we recognize we already were and
are.

There is nothing we have to do to be ourselves.

If we think we have been being ourselves all our lives, ask
yourself the following questions: "How happy are
you? How much joy and wealth have you? How
wonderful is your life? Do you have a fantastic
relationship?"

Not having all these is not being yourself—it is being
your NOT-self, your NOT-you.

When we are truly being ourselves, life is ecstatic.

The only question is, "How much more can I take? It is so
good, I cannot bear it! Money is pouring in and
everybody adores me!"

Being ourselves is exciting, fun, easy and free!

It is not hard work.

Hard work is a belief—the mind creates hard work.

We must look at the beliefs we have.

Once we know that we are the infinite space—just accept
this for the moment, you can go back to struggling
afterwards—everything is fine.

Accept that "I am just the space of this room. I am the
space and I notice that there are other objects or
bodies in this room—and they are all within me. I
contain them, *I am them.*"

ME LOOKING FROM
SEPARATION
TO OTHERS

I AM THE SPACE
CONTAINING THE
WHOLE

*My natural state is joyful, free, abundant, happy and full
of love."*

How come I do not feel this way?
If we can get to there and see this, we can then start
unpeeling ourselves.
We can look at the dynamics of how we have stopped and
limited ourselves through erroneous judgements and
beliefs.

We all know that we programme our minds through the
experiences that we have.
For example, if my mother leaves me during my childhood,
I have this traumatic experience and feel I have been
deserted, rejected and that no one loves me... and I
go through life with 'no one loves me'.
To everybody who comes and says, "I love you", you reply,
"No, you don't: that is absolutely impossible, because
no one loves me".
This is the subconscious level speaking, not in the surface
5% of our consciousness.

Heaven is down in the subconscious.

Yogis think that Heaven is above us when they find a samhadi and blissful state, but when they come back to the body, nothing has changed.

They have found a temporary Heaven, but not a permanent one.

Descend the other way, INTO the body.

The body is the temple, the place where we will find everything.

We will find the truth of our life in our body.

Every cell of our body contains the whole universe.

Everything ever known, thought or felt is contained in this body... YOUR body!

So there is no place we have to go except into our bodies to have our lives change.

I do not have to chase off to a mountaintop, because the truth of my life is right here.

If I want to move from sadness to happiness, from poverty
  to prosperity, to have joy, or to have a relationship
  when I do not have one, there is nowhere else I need
  to go except this body.

*It is all about my consciousness and relationship with
  me!*

All I have to do is peel away the unconsciousness.
When we hit some sub- or unconscious stuff, we bring it
  into consciousness, into the light of our awareness,
  so we can see it.
We can see it to be unresolved love, since everything is
  love.
As everything is love, all of our problems must be
  unresolved love, meaning they are parts of love.

If I am in pain, I am also in love ... I am just not aware of
  it.
I have had my intention on it being "bad", "wrong", rather
  than it is just showing me something about resolving
  myself and returning myself to the space that I am,
  the truth that I am ... and to love."

Every issue is a love issue.

Everything that is going on in our lives, where it is not
  turning out the way we truly want it to, is a love
  issue, an issue with ourselves.
These issues hold us from the truth of who we are.
We do not allow the real ecstasy into our lives, because
  we punish ourselves, blame ourselves and try to get
  things to ourselves, since we do not feel we are the
  centre.

There is a whole psychology about returning ourselves to
  a state of joy, peace and happiness.
It may seem that it must be a journey—but we can also
  step straight there.

47

All we need to do is give and receive love.

Usually we give judgement, criticism, grievances—all of the things that hold people apart from us.

The mind tries to separate all the pieces, to say there is not oneness, that there is a 'you' there doing it to 'me' here.

Every time we point the finger, we damage ourselves a bit more.

Every time we judge someone, we judge ourselves.

Unless we see divine love everywhere, we are limiting ourselves from the truth of our being.

Our work is finding the way of seeing that this is the truth.

I have the opportunity to change my thinking.

If I can change my thinking, my life changes, as life down here is experienced through the mind.

The *feeling* is who we are.

To have it turn out, we have to transform our thinking and our feeling.

We have to become aware of the feelings that we have.

There is only one feeling, and that is joy—all the other feelings are emotions, resistances and reactions.

If we are feeling anything other than supreme joy, then we are limiting ourselves.

Why let ourselves feel anger, hurt, resentment and bitterness, when joy is a much nicer feeling?

We feel other feelings, because the mind says, "You are separate!", "There is someone else over there doing it to you", or "It's God up there doing it to you".

We now want to find the way in which we can make the changes.

We recognize: "My life is the way it is, because I scripted it that way. I saw it through the lenses of my own mind. My perception of life is what I get. What I put out comes back. I intend it."

Our life is exactly the way we intend it to be; not necessarily the way we want it to be.
If our life is a certain way, for some reason we intend that.

If we can appreciate this, we can then decide: "I do not want it to be this way anymore. I want my life to move. I want to take a step. I would like to begin to feel joy, happiness and ease."

If we want to, we can start making this journey.
Instead of looking outwards "over there", judging the world and trying to fix the world up, we recognize that it is over here.

So now I go and feel my feelings and I look at my thoughts.
What is my thought, my belief, my attitude about anything—about, say, money? Is money the root of evil?"
If money is the root of evil, there is no wonder there is none in the bank... "I do not want to be evil, so if I have some I must be evil."

If I have no relationship, it must be that I intend not to have one.
Why would I do that, when I want one?
You do not have one, because you do not allow yourself one.
If we really allow a relationship, we will have that relationship.
We are our own worst enemies.

We can choose to give up our judgements on ourselves and truly love ourselves.

Judgements we have on ourselves are what we throw out
    on other people, because we cannot bear the pain of
    it over here.
If I can blame someone, I do not have to feel my pain.
If I were to feel it, and recognise that I have this
    judgement on myself, I see it in the mirror of life out
    here and I can make the change.
I can see how I have made myself wrong, and how I am
    punishing myself.

"When was the time that I made that decision?"
"When was the time that it hurt so much that I closed
    down?"
"When was the time that I hurt so much, that I never
    wanted to feel that pain again?"

"I have been avoiding that pain all of my life.
With amazing creativity, I will do anything, I will sabotage
    everything in my life, so that I do not have to feel
    that pain."

We wonder why we do not have the things we want.
We do not have the things we want, because when we get
    close to them, it is so painful we cannot stand it.
They remind us of something from our past.
If we accept reincarnation, it could even have been from a
    long way back.
The pain was so much that we made a decision which
    went into the computer of the mind.
Our decisions become operating principles in our lives
    from which we live.
If we want to change our operating principles, we go back
    and find out when we made those decisions and
    change them.

We have the power to change our decisions.
We can have what we want, or we can explain it and
have instead the reasons why we do not have what
we want.

People have plenty of reasons.
We can rationalize things any way we like, but it doesn't
make any difference.
If our life is not abundant, flowing and easy, there is
something to change, some decision we made,
someone to forgive, somewhere we have separated
ourselves.
We can only keep ourselves separate with pain and guilt.
We put resentment in the way to keep ourselves separate.
As there is only one, what I think my mother, father or
others did to me that I am resentful of, I did to them.
We give to others exactly what we think they are giving,
or doing, to us.

Many people do not believe that they could be like those
they are judging—they always think things were done
to them:
"I was only three when my father beat me. I could not
have done that!"
We may not have done the beating, but we made the
judgement.
We decided that someone else was bad or that we were
bad, and punished ourselves for it.

We go inside and begin to dig into the subconscious mind,
where we will find all of the things in our life that
are unresolved, all of the parts of ourselves which are
not in the oneness, all of the places we have
fractured ourselves.

We split ourselves and hold ourselves separate from
others with pain.
Pain and guilt give jealousy, judgement, grief—other forms
of feeling separate.

51

It is the separation which brings the grief.
Once we realize there is no separation, the grief
    disappears.

**There is only one life and that is the good life—the life
of the divine.**

The divine is a feeling of joy and happiness. So, if there is
    only one life, and it is divine, and I am not
    experiencing that, I must be separating myself from
    it.
No wonder everything is not flowing wonderfully, because
    there is some place where I am holding it from me,
    where I don't think I deserve it.
I do not think I deserve the love, the ease or the
    happiness I want.
I keep it away to prove my separation belief about myself.

*As we begin to dig down here, we find all of these
    fractured parts of ourselves.*

They show up in other people.
The people around us are the fractured parts which
    remind us.
We do not have to look anywhere else.

52

Families are wonderful—God put everybody together in a
family so that we could not escape each other.
You can run away from all sorts of people, but a family
will always follow you.
People sit in the Himalayas, change their names, deny
their families ever existed; but in spite of this
"escape" the fractured pieces remain fractured.

Move towards your family and heal the relationship.
Be yourself.
Go into the truth of yourself.
If you trust the universe, and trust that everything is fine,
everything turns out perfectly.

In fact, everything is perfect right now.

Even if we do not like it now, it is perfect feedback for us
about areas in ourselves we can change.
This is the perfection in the *im*perfection.

*If I were to move to love and ease, go into myself in
meditation, or just relax, to remind myself that
everything I see and think 'out there' is me, and
make the adjustments, what happens?*
*As we are all one, all connected, 'they' will begin to
move to the same space and we find that love
begins to return.*

As we heal ourselves, the world heals.
For every little bit that we gain in healing ourselves, we do
it for everyone, especially for our families and others
who are close to us.
Our healings also show up in the world: when enough
people have made these adjustments, major things
happen in life—like the Berlin Wall coming down, or
the superpowers moving from opposition into
partnership.
The world has taken some major steps and we can be
singing in the streets by the end of the century.

We do not have to dig concrete shelters.
Ten years ago we bought books on how to dig concrete
    shelters.
All of the training courses were on "How can we survive?"
People thought, "The world is fixed—it is an unchangeable
    place."
If this is the way you think, it is definitely going to be this
    way.
Our thoughts are creative—not the thought itself, that is
    just the mould.
We put our beingness into our thoughts and energize
    them and, guess what?—It shows up.

What we are afraid of happens, because that is what we
    have the most energy on.
Creation is thought filled with energy.
Creation is like baking a cake: you have the mould, put in
    all of the ingredients, cook it and get the right
    amount of energy in it and what happens?—A cake
    turns up!
It is the same in life.

You have a project, you have the right thought mould, you
    put the right amount of energy into it, and it turns
    up.
Creation, money and life happen through energizing our
    thoughts.

If we want changes in our life, we change our thoughts
    and energize them.
We have the power to change it to what we do want.
A girl I know who is convinced she will die in five days
    almost certainly will, unless she changes her thought
    to something else.

These are gifts we can give ourselves—we buy what we
    love to give as gifts . . . because they are gifts to
    ourself.
This is also true of the negative gifts.

54

We give ourselves lots of negative gifts in the beliefs about
    ourselves that limit us. So change them!
Just as there was nothing wrong with the girl who
    thought she was going to die, there is nothing wrong
    with you either.
So why do we have these thoughts that stop us from
    finding life so wonderful that we just do not know
    what to do with ourselves?

What are the changes we could make?
What are the areas of our life which are not really the
    way we would like them to be?
What are the beliefs we have about money?
Do I judge other people who have money?
What do I think about my father, or about business?
Do I think I have stolen money, and therefore judge
    myself and do not allow myself to have any?
What are the judgements that I have which are stopping
    things flowing in my life?

When our energy is high, things happen and everything
    begins to flow.
What are my judgements on relationship?
Who am I judging and making wrong?
It is all me I am making wrong!
If all the time I am condemning me, how can anybody
    have or want a relationship with all the
    condemnation?
If I do not have a relationship, it is because I do not
    believe I deserve one.
It is not that you have to go out and grab someone, but
    simply move in the direction of your life.
If we move in the direction of the truth of our life,
    everything else will follow us.

Do not use other people to hold yourself back.
Do not try to sort others out.
Move to the truth of your being and the true ones will
    come with you.
The others will be true to someone else.

There is a perfect order to the universe, if we would only get out of the way.

The universe works perfectly well.—Could we manage it better? . . . the flow of the tides, the sun coming up at the right time, or the flowers blooming when they do . . .?
Is there anyone who could do these things with their mind?
Could we even create a flower with our mind?
Why are we so arrogant to think that we can do it with our minds?

The age of the mind is coming to an end.
The age of intuition is here.
It is the age of inspiration, of being, of taking a step, and of moving nearer to the truth of our being.
It becomes easier as we listen to intuition—the voice of the universe between our thoughts.
It is not based on past recordings in our mind.
Past recordings are reason, based on past information, which is only part of what is really going on.
Intuition knows the whole picture.
Knowing the whole of it, we can take a step forward and trust that our life will move and flow in the direction that is for our highest good.

It takes our willingness to make that shift.
When we take that step towards each other, we find that all of the pain we have between us begins to melt, transforms into love, and we begin to enjoy that unity.
Unity is not bodies tied together.
Unity is the space that contains and is the whole.
As we begin to transform our thoughts, and truly feel our feelings again (and Western man has not really felt his feelings—he has usually reacted), we know that under those feelings is the truth.
Under these feelings is the joy we want.

56

The key is to feel our feelings with our consciousness, our
   awareness, and let them transform and burn, but
   move through them and towards each other with trust.

If we live in trust, the universe will serve us.
If we live in doubt, that is the way it will be for us.

You cannot describe God, because God is not of the mind,
   the machine of reason.
God is best experienced through feeling.
As we begin to go with feelings we find deeper aspects of
   It.
Our deepest pain is probably our closest moment to
   Heaven.
The extremes get us nearer.
In the deepest unconsciousness in the cells we will find
   the divine.
The nineties is the age of transformation.
For the next century we move to a whole new level of
   consciousness.

Mastery is so easy that everything happens—the universe
   responds to our every wish.
Everything that is separate from us we heal through our
   hearts—not by force, but by integration, the way of
   love.
Bring into your hearts everybody and everything you feel
   separate from.

"INTEGRATING PEOPLE IN YOUR HEART"

BROTHERS · CHILDREN · BILL · MOTHER · BOSS · AUNT LILLY · THE GOUERNMENT · DOCTORS · GEORGE · FATHER · SISTER AGNES · MARY · TEACHERS · TOM · PRIESTS · SISTER · GRANDPARENTS · THE CHURCH

Meditation

I acknowledge that I am the source of my own
      wellbeing.
I acknowledge that only good things can happen in my
      life if I acknowledge that I have first created them
      in myself.

I let go my judgements of everybody and heal the
      uncomfortable feelings I have towards them from
      within myself with love.

I love them unconditionally the way they are ... AS I DO
      MYSELF.

I let my energies come together with the energies of
      those around me in a loving way ... And in a way
      that supports our aliveness.

I give out to others all the things I want for
      myself ... And I open to receiving them in return.

I recognize that coming into a loving alignment with
      other people opens me to my inexhaustible well of
      plenty.

MORE LIFE-ENHANCING MATERIAL
from
WELLSPRING PUBLICATIONS

Additional Books By Shaun de Warren

YOU ARE THE KEY
A Guide to Self-Discovery

24 Chapters include: * Why Suffer? *Clues to Self Healing *
Meditation * Prosperity * Intuition * Relationships * How to
Dissolve Attitudes * Dreams * The Spiritual Dimension

"Shaun describes his book as "Holding the vision of Oneness and
assisting people to manage their lives in all aspects from this
viewpoint and with joy and ease. A wonderful book of spiritual
exposition and one which I would ardently recommend"

—Brian Graham. Science of Thought Review

THE MIRROR OF LIFE
Your Adventure in Self-Discovery

The sequel and companion volume to "YOU ARE THE KEY", this
book takes you further along the path of self-discovery and
lightness.
"It's interesting to watch 'out there' to find out about
ourselves ... I radiate thoughts that are bouncing back in the
mirror of life so that I can see them ... The fascinating thing is
that if we make our adjustments here in what we see 'over there'
we find that 'over there' changes"

Also includes * The Nature of Being * Individual Sovereignty *
Lifescripting * Steps to Prosperity * Laughter * Sex *
Transforming Relationships * Be Good To Yourself * The Sound
Current * Barriers to Being * Healing Family Karma * Beyond
Good and Evil

THE HANDBOOK SERIES

Richly bound in gold-embossed hard covers, these pocket-size books contain aphorisms chosen to encourage true prosperity, happy and loving relationships and abundant health. An ideal gift for yourself or to give to others

THE PROSPERITY HANDBOOK

Gems to Enrich Your Life, Pocket and Consciousness

THE RELATIONSHIPS HANDBOOK

Jewels to Bring Love and Happiness

THE HEALTH HANDBOOK

Pearls to Inspire Healing

OTHER WELLSPRING TITLES

AWAKEN THE GODS

Aphorisms to Remember the Way Home

Chuck Spezzano Ph.D

THE 10-DAY BROWN RICE DIET

A Journey Toward Inner and Outer Well Being

Sue Lake and Susan Mayne

TAPES

This selection of tapes are recorded lectures by
Shaun de Warren. Each tape is 90 minutes long unless
otherwise noted

A VISION OF PROSPERITY

When we learn to live in our Vision of Prosperity, many
new avenues are awakened and our prosperity expands in
every way. This tape leads us in discovering our personal
prosperity and a global vision

YOU CAN HAVE ABUNDANCE

Specific ways in which we can have more abundance in our
lives. An ideal complement to A VISION OF PROSPERITY

LOVE AND ABUNDANCE

Aspects of Dr Chuck Spezzano's sacred psychology are
highlighted and explored in this tape to show our journey
from dependence through independence and into
partnership, love and happiness

TAPPING INTO YOUR INEXHAUSTBLE
WELL OF PLENTY

Specific tips on rediscovering your natural state of joy,
freedom, abundance, happiness and love, showing that you
have the power to make choices, change decisions and have
what you want

IT'S TIME TO LIVE YOUR DREAMS

Now's the time! You don't need to wait until tomorrow,
next week, next month or next year...

A complete list of books and tapes is available from
Wellspring Publications at the address below.

If you have difficulty in obtaining any of the above
materials and/or would like details about courses, lectures
and consultations by Shaun de Waren, please contact

WELLSPRING PUBLICATIONS LIMITED

46 Cyril Mansions, Prince of Wales Drive,
London SW11 4HW, U.K.